THE DVD BOOK OF
DOGS

Written by Jon Stroud

This edition first published in the UK in 2008
By Green Umbrella Publishing

© Green Umbrella Publishing 2008

www.gupublishing.co.uk

Publishers Jules Gammond & Vanessa Gardner

Printed and bound in China

ISBN 978-1-905828-51-7

THE DVD BOOK OF
DOGS

Contents

CONTENTS

A Dogs World – A Brief History

THE DOG, AS WE WOULD RECOGnise it today, has been with us for somewhere between 14,000 to 17,000 years. Even in those earliest of times there existed a relationship between man and *Canis lupus familiaris*. It was first thought that these early dogs' ancestors were jackals but more recent thinking, aided and abetted by DNA sampling, suggests that it was *Canis lupus pallipes* – a small type of grey wolf that was prevalent across North America, Europe and Asia which, although it is still found in Iran, Afghanistan and Pakistan, is now endangered.

There are various theories regarding the origins of the domestic dog. A popular suggestion is that wolves who scavenged from rubbish pits near to ancient habitations gradually became accustomed to their human hosts having realised that those who fled the least ate the best. Since the earliest known domestication, said to have taken place between 12,000 and 10,000BC, the size, shape and the role of dogs in society has changed dramatically.

Five distinct types of dogs have existed since at least the early Bronze Age. The largest of these are the Mastiffs or Molossers (*Canis familiaris inostranzewi*) – a superheavyweight known to have been domesticated in Tibet in the Stone Age and later bred extensively in Greece and the Balkans. There was the *Canis familiaris leineri* – a harrier-

type resembling the modern-day greyhound known to have existed in Mesopotamia 8,000 years ago – from which the *Canis familiaris intermedius*, the braque or pointer type dogs used for the hunting of game, were developed. *Canis familiaris metris-optimae*, the sheep herders and cattle drovers, have worked with and protected livestock from predators, often other canines, for many thousands of years. The final types, the *Canis familiaris palustris*, were wolf-like breeds similar to the Siberian Husky.

The place of the dog in human history is well documented. During the Peloponnesian War in the fifth century BC, the mighty citadel at Corinth was

guarded by 50 dogs placed outside of the walls on the seashore. One night, besieging forces killed 49 of them in one attack. The sole survivor, Soter, ran to the city gates to warn the Corinthians and, in the process, saved the lives of many citizens. He was honoured with a silver collar engraved "Soter, defender and preserver of Corinth". His slaughtered companions were also remembered through a magnificent marble statue.

The Romans famously took dogs with them on their conquering campaigns across Europe, Asia and the north of Africa. These dogs were extensively bred with other local breeds spreading and diversifying bloodlines throughout the Empire. As with their horse stock, to the Romans the breeding and the training of their dogs was a highly important matter. They were utilised as hunters, guardians, herders and drovers with careful breeding used to accentuate and fine tune the specific characteristics needed. Then, during the fourth century AD, invading forces and merchant traders from Asia brought with them many new types of dog interbreeding from which introduced a whole host of new traits including the curly coat that is now prevalent in so many breeds.

The fall of the once mighty Roman Empire also signified a decline in the importance of dog breeding. Life was hard, disease was rife and war was plentiful. Things were not looking good for the humble canine however its fortunes were saved by its unparalleled skill in the hunting field. Monasteries all across Europe were quick to recognise that dog breeding could offer a healthy income as the wealthy feudal nobility clamoured for quality animals to accompany them on the hunt. This led to the rise of many of the hunting dogs whose ancestry can be seen in countless breeds today such as the Bloodhound and the Beagle.

The Emperors of China had their Lion Dogs, Charles I of England had his Spaniels, Marie Antoinette had her Papillon – even Queen Elizabeth II has her beloved Welsh Corgis.

For many years it has been commonplace for the ruler of a country to own a canine companion.

It is, however, a little more unusual for a dog to have served as a monarch!

In the eleventh century, Onund, the son of Norway's King Eystein the Great was placed in charge of the region of Throndhjem but, after a period of unrest, he was over thrown and killed.

Eystein retook the kingdom and offered its people a choice – if they were not to be ruled by him they could either be governed by his slave, Thorer Faxe, or his trusty dog Suening.

They chose the dog. Eystein demanded that Suening should be offered the station, rights and privileges befitting a king.

He was given a collar fashioned from gold and silver, his own throne and was carried on the shoulders of courtiers whenever he travelled.

Like Eystein's unfortunate son, Suening eventually met a bloody end.

His demise, however, had nothing to do with any form of insurgency – despite his royal status he had refused to give up his day job and was killed whilst bravely defending his herd of cattle against a raging pack of wolves.

Over the centuries, a good dog became an expensive commodity and took on a new found role as a status symbol for wealthy nobles and merchants and for the first time canines were kept purely as companions. Kings not only owned dogs but also gave them as gifts and, once again, the bloodlines spread and the breeds diver-

attentions to turn to the somewhat less vociferous pastime of showing.

Although various sorts of unofficial dog show had taken place in pubs and at country fairs across the country for many years, the first official dog show was held in the Town Hall, Newcastle upon Tyne, in June 1859. Only setters and pointers took part but an impressive 60 entries were put forward for judging. Later that same year, a gamekeeper by the name of Richard Brailsford organised another show in the galleries of the Birmingham Horse and Carriage Repository. It was a hugely successful event with 80 dogs entered across the 14 different classes. This event, the National Dog Show, is still contested to this day.

For several years two bodies controlled the administration of dog shows in the United Kingdom – the National Dog Club and the National Dog Society. Whilst both organisations performed their task admirably, by 1870 it was seen as desirable to form a single body to administer all canine matters. On 4 April 1873, following a meeting of 12 gentlemen at 2 Albert Mansions, Victoria Street, London, the Kennel Club was formed. Eleven years later, in the rooms of the Philadelphia Kennel Club, the

sified even further.

The establishment of new breeds reached a new high in the eighteenth and nineteenth century when both specialist types were created and previously lost ancient breeds were recreated. They were developed for rural and field work such as herding, pointing and retrieving, urban tasks like ratting and for less salubrious activities such as fighting and bear-baiting. In the United Kingdom, the 1835 Cruelty to Animals Act ostensibly put an end to these barbaric acts allowing

United States followed suit with the formation of the American Kennel Club.

Whilst the twentieth century has seen companion-dog ownership go from strength to strength, it has also witnessed even more dogs being utilised for their unique working skills. In the First World War, canines were used extensively as messengers, guards and even for locating the wounded. They have been employed by police and security services across the world as sniffers, trackers and for their rather effective ability to show a sharp set of teeth and a resounding bark when required. They have helped the blind see and the deaf hear. They have even been into space. With over 10 millennia of combined history there can be no doubt that man and dog share a unique and special bond and with ownership ever on the increase it is a relationship that looks set to stay. Looking after a dog is not always the easiest of things to do but it is certainly one of the most rewarding.

Gundogs

THE GUNDOG GROUP ENCOMP-asses a selection of breeds that were originally developed to assist hunters by tracking, pointing or retrieving a quarry. The group is basically split into three principal categories:

Spaniels

TAKEN FROM THE OLD FRENCH term espagneul, meaning Spanish dog, the spaniel is an intelligent, medium sized dog that is optimised for hunting and retrieving in rough and over-grown country. They generally have an excellent sense of smell, tough thorn-proof coats and long, protective ears. In the field, the spaniel tends to work fairly close to the gun to flush out prey which it will then retrieve on com-mand. In addition to the traditional hunting breeds there are some vari-eties, such as the American Cocker Spaniel which are now essentially a toy or show breed.

Pointers and Setters

LARGER AND MORE ATHLETIC IN appearance are the pointers and setters – both of which tend to work well ahead of the guns. On scenting or spotting their prey, these breeds freeze to the spot and then point by raising a foreleg and stretching their muzzle in the direction of the quarry. The types vary in that the pointer will remain in this position whilst the setter will lie down, or set, as the hunter flushes the game.

Retrievers

BIG AND STRONG, THE RETRIEVER'S job is to stay close to the guns before being sent out to find and recover the game after it has been shot. They are frequently used in conjunction with spaniels who will first find and flush out the quarry.

Labrador Retriever

Labrador Retriever		
Breed Group	Gundog	
Height	Bitch	55 – 56cm
	Male	56 – 57cm
Weight	Bitch	28kg
	Male	30kg
Lifespan	9 – 15 years	

UNQUESTIONABLY BRITAIN'S MOST popular breed, the Labrador Retriever is renowned for its intelligence, loyalty and gentle nature making it the ideal choice for families with young children. However, it is not just as a family pet where the Labrador excels.

Originating in Newfoundland where it was used by fishermen to recover their nets from the freezing waters of the North Atlantic, the breed arrived in the United Kingdom in the early nineteenth century when it was recognised as a proficient gundog although it was not until 1887 that the Earl of Malmesbury coined the name Labrador. In addition to gundog duties the modern Labrador is frequently put to work by the police to sniff out illegal drugs whilst others find work as guide–dogs for the blind.

Adult Labradors are well built with a broad chest, level topline and powerful

Fun Facts

Former United States President Bill Clinton has two chocolate Labradors named Buddy and Seamus whilst past Russian President Vladimir Putin has a black one called Koni!

hindquarters. Its head is similarly broad with a pronounced stop and brow whilst its eyes, which can be brown or hazel, lend the breed an intelligent kindly expression. Waterborne propulsion is assisted by the breed's webbed toes whilst its strong, thick otter–like tail acts as a highly efficient rudder. Labradors can be black, yellow or chocolate in colour.

Weimaraner

WITH A DISTINCTIVE, IRIDESCENT silver grey coat, piercing blue or amber eyes and majestic, noble appearance the Weimaraner is a truly unique breed. Also known as the Grey Ghost it is the largest of the gundog group with the male growing as large as 69cm and weighing in at a hefty 32kg. Immensely

Fun Facts

Always at the forefront of popular culture, Weimaraners have featured on album covers for artists as diverse as Kate Bush and The Pogues.

graceful in motion, the Weimaraner is capable of showing a remarkable level of speed and endurance. This, coupled with a naturally inquisitive nature, makes for an animal that requires a considerable level of exercise to offset any destructive tendencies caused through boredom.

Nobody is quite certain of the precise origins of this breed – a remarkably similar looking creature can be seen in a 1631 painting by Van Dyke – although it is thought that the Weimaraner's genes may well hark back to the German Shorthaired Pointer, the German Schweisshund and the Bloodhound.

Taking its regal name from the house of Charles Augustus, Grand Duke of Saxe–Weimar–Eisenach, it was originally bred to hunt deer, wolves and bear but as the larger game breeds disappeared from Europe in the late nineteenth century it found a new lease of life as a highly efficient bird dog. Weimaraners are exceptionally loyal, enjoy company and make good family pets.

Weimaraner		
Breed Group	Gundog	
Height	Bitch	56 – 64cm
	Male	61 – 69cm
Weight	Bitch	22.5kg
	Male	27kg
Lifespan	10 – 12 years	

English Cocker Spaniel

English Cocker Spaniel		
Breed Group	Gundog	
Height	Bitch	38 – 39cm
	Male	39 – 41cm
Weight	Bitch	13kg
	Male	13kg
Lifespan	10 – 14 years	

A TRUE CLASSIC SPORTING BREED, the English Cocker Spaniel's heritage can be traced back as far as fourteenth century Castilian Spain. Originally all land spaniels were considered to be a single breed with smaller animals being utilised to flush out woodcock and larger ones being employed to spring game. It is from here that the names Cocker and Springer Spaniel are derived.

Showing exceptional alertness, intelligence and a biddable nature, the English Cocker Spaniel still holds its own in the field but has proved equally suitable as a friendly and loyal family pet. Sturdy and compact in build they boast a smooth and silky medium length coat that comes in a multitude of colours from solid blacks, reds and browns through combinations, roans and even tricolours.

As with any of the gundog group the English Cocker Spaniel demands a reasonable amount of exercise to stimulate its mind and expel excess energies and will relish the opportunity to dive into any convenient pond, stream or river for a refreshing swim.

Fun Facts

With seven titles to its name, the English Cocker Spaniel has won the title of Crufts Supreme Champion more than any other breed.

English Springer Spaniel

LIKE ITS COCKER SPANIEL COUSIN, the English Springer Spaniel's roots can be traced back over almost 700 years but it was not until the mid nineteenth century that selective breeding brought us the breed as we know it today. It was finally recognised by the Kennel Club of Great Britain in 1902 but took an addi-tional 25 years to gain acceptance from the American Kennel Club.

The Springer is often considered to be the most adaptable and robust of the hunting spaniels. Naturally per-ceptive and armed with a tremen-dously sensitive nose it has proved itself to be highly skilled on land or in the water excelling as a pointer, a retriever and as an expert flusher out of birds. Biddable, enthusiastic and always eager to please, it is quick to learn and generally easy to control making it an ideal choice as a family pet.

Medium sized, compact and well proportioned the Springer Spaniel's medium length flat or wavy coat offers a remarkable level of protection being not only weatherproof but water-proof and thorn resistant. The Springer can be black and white or liver and white in colour or, with the addition of tan markings, tricolour.

Fun Facts

In 2003 a Springer Spaniel named Buster serving with the Duke of Wellington's Regiment in Iraq received the Dickin Medal, the animal equivalent of the Victoria Cross, after discovering an insurgent group's cache of hidden weapons and explosives.

English Springer Spaniel

Breed Group	Gundog	
Height	Bitch	48 – 50cm
	Male	49 – 51cm
Weight	Bitch	23kg
	Male	24kg
Lifespan	9 – 15 years	

Golden Retriever

Golden Retriever		
Breed Group	Gundog	
Height	Bitch	51 – 56cm
	Male	56 – 61cm
Weight	Bitch	30kg
	Male	32kg
Lifespan	12 – 16 years	

THERE ARE FEW CREATURES THAT show more enthusiasm for a refreshing swim than the Golden Retriever. Bred originally for the hunting of wildfowl it boasts a thick, waterproof undercoat beneath a wavy or flat outer coat – one that must regularly be trimmed and groomed if it is to be kept in tip–top condition.

Fun Facts

Augie, a Golden Retriever owned by the Miller family of Dallas, Texas, holds the world record for the most tennis balls held in the mouth of a dog at one time having held five regulation sized balls in 2003!

The development of the Golden Retriever was essentially the work of Dudley Marjoribanks, 1st Baron Tweedmouth, who, in 1865, acquired from a Brighton cobbler a dog by the name of Nous – the only yellow coated puppy in a litter of otherwise black Wavy–Coated Retrievers that had been bred by the Earl of Chichester. Several years later he bred Nous to a Tweed Water Spaniel (now an extinct breed) called Belle. Belle produced four bitches – Ada, Cowslip, Crocus and Primrose – that form the basis of the Golden Retriever we know today.

Gentle to the extreme, patient, loyal

and confident they are an ideal family pet but require a good amount of exercise to keep them fit and in peak condition. Such is their desire to retrieve, they will almost always attempt to carry anything they can get hold of and returning owners can invariably expect to be the recipient of a gift of some nature.

Pointer

THE POINTER HAS, FOR MANY centuries, been regarded by many as the classic sporting dog. Sleek, noble and athletic it has long proved its versatility in retrieving both on land and from the water. It's key and most obvious trait is, however, the point itself – a motionless, elegant stance with one foreleg raised, tail run flat and head extended towards its prey.

There are several breeds of pointer in existence today but all can trace their lineage back to the Spanish Pointer which was introduced into Germany in the seventeenth century and England in the eighteenth century. Breeding with the English Foxhound and the Greyhound gave rise to the deep–chested and powerful English Pointer (now known simply as the

Pointer). In Germany, Spanish Pointers were cross bred with German hounds and Bloodhounds but it was not until bloodlines from English Pointer stock were introduced that the breed began to resemble what has now become the German Shorthaired and more latterly the German Longhaired Pointers.

Pointers are gentle, intelligent and obedient by nature and love to give and receive plenty of love and attention from their owners making them exceptional, if rather large, family pets. It should, however, always be remembered that they are bred for an outdoors life and, as such, require a substantial level of exercise.

Fun Facts

Ship's Dog Judy, an English Pointer, was the only animal to have officially been a POW in the Second World War and was awarded the Dickin Medal for "magnificent courage and endurance in Japanese prison camps, which helped to maintain morale among prisoners and for saving lives through her intelligence and watchfulness".

Pointer		
Breed Group	Gundog	
Height	Bitch	60 – 62cm
	Male	63 – 66cm
Weight	Bitch	32kg
	Male	30kg
Lifespan	12 – 15 years	

Hungarian Vizsla

Hungarian Vizsla		
Breed Group	Gundog	
Height	Bitch	53 – 60cm
	Male	57 – 64cm
Weight	Bitch	20 – 30kg
	Male	20 – 30kg
Lifespan	14 – 15 years	

BOASTING A UNIQUE RUSSET GOLD coat, the graceful Hungarian Vizsla is truly a member of the canine aristocracy for, until the First World War, their breeding was restricted to the nobility of the Greater Hungarian Kingdom. Only a select few outside of the nation were bestowed with the honour of receiving one as a gift. Its lineage, however, can be traced back considerably further to the times of the great Magyar hunters over 1000 years ago. The Vizsla all but died out during the ravages of the Second World War but it is thought that a handful of the animals were smuggled into Austria where the breed line was carefully maintained to safely secure its future.

A superb all–round medium sized

Fun Facts

The Hungarian Vizsla is one of just seven recognised HPR breeds – those that hunt, point and retrieve. The others are the German Shorthaired, Wirehaired and Longhaired Pointers, the Weimaraner, the Large Munsterlander, and the Italian Spinone.

hunting dog that excels in tracking, pointing and retrieving the Hungarian Vizsla is intelligent, obedient and not particularly difficult to train. Affectionate and, invariably, a lover of children it is an excellent choice as a family pet. However, owners should be aware that, whilst the Vizsla is equally at home in rural or urban surroundings, it will always require a considerable level of exercise.

Irish Setter

THE IRISH SETTER, ALSO WIDELY known as the Red Setter, is a popular breed that has taken the title of Crufts

Irish Setter		
Breed Group	Gundog	
Height	Bitch	64 – 69cm
	Male	64 – 69cm
Weight	Bitch	26kg
	Male	30.5kg
Lifespan	13 years +	

Supreme Champion on four occasions. The oldest of the setters, predating both the Gordon and English varieties, it is long legged, has a deceptively muscular build and, most obviously, a highly distinctive silky coat that can be rich chestnut or even dark mahogany in colour.

Although developed originally for hunting, the Irish Setter's playful and mischievous nature can often prove a distraction – away from the field and in a domestic setting this can occasionally prove a challenge as they have a tendency to want to remain detached from the lead if ever given the chance. With this in mind rigorous obedience training is a must early in a setter's life although the breed is known to retain a puppyish nature throughout its adult life.

Calmer and more considered in temperament is the Gordon Setter – the largest and strongest of the group. Originally bred by the Duke of Gordon on his Scottish estate it possesses a wonderful medium length black and tan coat said to be inherited from a Collie forebear. The English Setter is distinguished by speckled (or bel-ton) coat. Always white in ground the flecks may be black (blue belton), orange, lemon or liver in colour.

Fun Facts

In February 2008 a two year old Irish Setter bitch gave birth to an astonishing litter of 16 puppies in Terrington St Clement, Norfolk. And the key to her prolific brood? A diet of battered cod and chips!

Hounds

earliest examples of man and dog working in harmony. In fact, evidence exists of such animals being used in the Middle East as early as 6000BC and the great Greek historian Arrian makes mention of their use in Europe in the second century AD.

PROVIDING SPEED AND A KEEN sense of smell and sight, hounds were the very first form of hunting dog used by man. They can be split into two basic categories:

Sight hounds

SIGHT HOUNDS OR GAZE HOUNDS are those which primarily rely on their hawk–like vision to locate a quarry before using their speed and stealth to launch a pursuit. These are truly the

Scent Hounds

DEVELOPED IN EUROPE DURING the early Middle Ages, scent hounds track game by using the nose to locate ground scents. Strong and robust they do not require the flat–out speed of the sight hound as they have no need to keep a target constantly in view – instead they make use of their immense stamina to gradually wear down their prey. A long muzzle helps in keeping the nose close to the ground whilst a large pair of pendulous ears keeps any scent close to the dog's face.

Afghan Hound

SOMETIMES KNOWN AS THE KABUL Dog, the Tazi or the Baluchi, this ancient breed's origins can be traced back to a handful of North African sight hounds that were taken via trading routes to the mountains of Afghanistan over 4,000 years ago. Those with the thickest, heaviest coats were selectively bred to produce

a hardy, athletic creature that excelled as a companion to hunters and shepherds alike that showed exceptional bravery and a willingness to take on even the most ferocious beasts single handed.

Originally the export of Afghan Hounds was forbidden however, after the relaxation of regulations, the first animal, named Zardin, arrived in the United Kingdom in the early part of the twentieth century as the property of a Captain Banff who proceeded to show it to great acclaim at the Crystal Palace Kennel Club Show in 1907.

Despite being exceptionally intelligent the Afghan Hound can prove to be a stubborn and difficult dog to train and it is essential that all of the basics are taught at a very early age. They are, however, very affectionate and show a great deal of loyalty to their owners – who, in turn, must be prepared to return this affection by providing a substantial daily program of exercise and regular laborious grooming sessions.

Afghan Hound		
Breed Group	Hound	
Height	Bitch	63 – 69cm
	Male	68 – 74cm
Weight	Bitch	24kg
	Male	27kg
Lifespan	14 years +	

Basset Hound

Basset Hound		
Breed Group	Hound	
Height	Bitch	33 – 38cm
	Male	33 – 38cm
Weight	Bitch	18 – 27kg
	Male	18 – 27kg
Lifespan	12 years +	

THE FAITHFUL BASSET HOUND IS A big dog with a big heart – but oh–so short legs! But this is not to denigrate this wonderful breed for it is exactly these characteristics which have made the humble Basset one of the most useful hunting dogs of all time. Boasting a superlative sense of smell and a tenacious nature, they were first bred by French monks during the Middle Ages to hunt in heavy cover – their name being derived from the French word bas meaning low.

It was, however, not until the latter half of the nineteenth century that the breed really flourished having been imported to the United Kingdom by Lord Galway. Selective breeding led to the establishment of an outstanding pack which formed the basis of the English version of the breed we know today.

Despite its melancholy appearance,

Fun Facts

Alex Graham's comic strip character Fred Basset has appeared in the Daily Mail newspaper since 1963. In Germany he is called Wurzel whilst in Finland he is known as Pitko.

the Basset can be a sociable and playful creature with a mischievous sense of humour. They get on exceptionally well with children and other household pets but have a mind of their own and can be a chore to train. Although they invariably display a lethargic nature, exercise should never be overlooked as they easily gain weight which can lead to the development of back problems.

Beagle

Beagle		
Breed Group	Hound	
Height	Bitch	33 – 40cm
	Male	33 – 40cm
Weight	Bitch	8 – 14kg
	Male	8 – 14kg
Lifespan	12 – 15 years	

ONE OF THE SMALLEST OF THE hunting hounds, the Beagle is another breed whose origins can be traced to France. Brought to England in 1066 by the Norman conquerors its name is said to have been derived from the term begueule meaning "open throat" – a reference to the breed's somewhat musical inclinations! Due to its strong hunting instincts, a Beagle can take time and patience to train and should only be let off of its lead once the owner can be absolutely certain it will return on command – once a Beagle has locked onto a scent it is unlikely it will return voluntarily. They are expert escape artists and can make light work of an apparently secure garden by scaling walls and digging their way under fences. They are, however, sociable, cheerful and extremely good natured and will get on well with other dogs and with their human pack.

Measuring just over 22cm to the shoulder, an even smaller variety known as the Pocket Beagle was developed so that it could be carried around in a rider's saddlebags. Extinct for many years it has now been recreated and is being bred once more.

Dachshund

Dachshund		
Breed Group	Hound	
Chest Girth*	Miniature	20 – 35cm
	Standard	35cm +
Weight	Bitch	9 – 12kg
	Male	9 – 12kg
Lifespan	9 – 15 years	

*Uniquely Dachshunds are measured not by height but by chest girth.

"HALF A DOG HIGH AND A DOG-an-a-half long" was how Baltimore essayist H L Mencken described the plucky little Dachshund. Heralding from sixteenth century Germany they were originally bred and trained to chase down foxes and badgers (Dachshund actually means "Badger Dog") by entering a set or lair before killing and then retrieving the prey – a far cry from the often belittling title of "sausage dog" awarded the brave Dachshund in this day and age.

There are six separate Dachshund breeds currently recognised – long–haired, smooth–haired and wire–haired each in both standard and miniature form. All are essentially the same except for their coat variety and overall size. Due to its naturally curious nature, a Dachsie can often be difficult to train – its thoroughly active mind being easily diverted to more interesting pursuits. Dachshunds tend to be very dominant even with much larger breeds of dog and if berated can often sulk for extended periods of time before rejoining the family group. It is,

however, on the whole a very friendly little breed that can become very attached to particular family members.

An additional benefit to ownership is that, with an alert mind and a piercingly loud bark, they can single handedly replace the household burglar alarm in one fell swoop.

Fun Facts

A Dachshund named Waldi was the first Olympic mascot and symbol of the 1972 Summer Olympics in Munich.

Greyhound

THE GREYHOUND IS AN ANCIENT breed whose image can be seen engraved on the tombs of many Egyptian and African kings dating back to 4000BC. Having probably arrived with Phoenician traders their popularity gradually spread across Europe as they became recognised as possessing an unmatched ability to course large game such as wolves, deer and antelopes. On arrival in England they were accorded such a high status that King Canute himself proclaimed the "no meane person may keep any greyhounds" – quite simply they were considered such expert hunters that only noblemen were considered worthy of ownership.

The Greyhound acquired its name not from the colour but from the Saxon word grei, meaning beautiful or fine. This is an appropriate term indeed, for the Greyhound is a supremely elegant creature. The most athletic of all canines, its hugely powerful body and long, strong, muscular legs can propel it from standstill to a top speed in excess of 64 km/h (40mph) in a little over two seconds taking no more than six strides to do so.

Although most commonly found on the racetrack, the Greyhound makes an excellent family pet being sensitive, loving and very well behaved. Considering their size they have a relatively small appetite and require little exercise – a couple of 20 minute walks per day are more than sufficient. Care should, however, be taken in public places as it will naturally chase anything it sees moving.

Fun Facts

The Greyhound is the only canine mentioned by name in the King James Bible – "There be three things which go well, yea, four are comely in going: A lion which is strongest among beasts, and turneth not away for any; A greyhound; an he goat also; and a king, against whom there is no rising up." – Proverbs 30:29–31.

Greyhound		
Breed Group	Hound	
Height	Bitch	68 – 71cm
	Male	71 – 76cm
Weight	Bitch	29kg
	Male	31kg
Lifespan	10 – 12 years	

Irish Wolfhound

Irish Wolfhound		
Breed Group	Hound	
Height	Bitch	71cm +
	Male	79cm +
Weight	Bitch	26kg +
	Male	30.5kg +
Lifespan	6 – 9 years	

THE IMPRESSIVE AND IMPOSING Irish Wolfhound is a giant amongst dogs. Before being brought to Irish shores, its greyhound ancestors were crossed with rangy mastiffs whilst travelling across the plains of Europe with the conquering Celts in the third century BC. Expert in the pursuit of wild boar, elk and wolves and as guard dogs, they found favour with the rich and noble to a point where, in the seventeenth century, Oliver Cromwell had to prohibit their export from British shores. After the last Irish wolf was killed in the late 1700s the Wolfhound decreased in numbers to a point where it almost became extinct however, thanks to the efforts of army officer Captain George Graham, its future was secured in the second half of the nineteenth century.

As a pet, the Wolfhound is friendly, exceptionally loyal and loves children (no, not to eat!) however, care should be taken in play as these gentle giants can often forget how big and strong they really are. As with many of the extra large breeds they require relatively little exercise.

The most famous Irish Wolfhound is, undoubtedly, Gelert. He was the property of Llewelyn, a thirteenth century Prince of North Wales. One day as he left for the

hunt Gelert was inexplicably absent. On Llewelyn's return, the hound excitedly appeared once more to greet his master but with his jaws and coat soaked red with blood. The prince ran to find his son only to find an empty bloodstained cot. He drew his sword and plunged it deep into the hound's chest however, as he did so, he heard a child's cry. He searched again and found his son completely safe and unharmed – next to it was the savaged body of an enormous wolf which Gelert had slain to protect the child.

> ### Fun Facts
>
> *The Irish Wolfhound is a breed with its own motto! "Gentle when stroked. Fierce when provoked."*

Rhodesian Ridgeback

Rhodesian Ridgeback		
Breed Group	Hound	
Height	Bitch	61 – 66cm
	Male	63 – 67cm
Weight	Bitch	30 – 39kg
	Male	30 – 39kg
Lifespan	12 years	

THE RHODESIAN RIDGEBACK OF today resulted from the crossing of various breeds such as mastiffs and deerhounds, imported by Boer settlers to South Africa in the sixteenth and seventeenth centuries, with the Khoikhoi dog – an indigenous breed notable for its unique line of hair growing along its spine in the reverse direction to the rest of its coat. Its full name was only derived after the breed standard was set in Rhodesia (now Zimbabwe) in 1922.

It proved ideal for the tough conditions of the African Veld, earning favour as a guard and protector and as an expert hunter capable of tracking quarry and retrieving. Made of hardy stock it copes easily with the varied extremes of the bush which can drop close to zero overnight but climb to temperatures in excess of 40C in the midday sun. Used in packs, the Rhodesian Ridgeback can prove a formidable adversary for buffalo or any of

Fun Facts

A Rhodesian Ridgeback can go for over 24 hours without needing water and is almost impervious to insect bites.

the big cats – for this reason it is also widely known as the African Lion Hound or the Rhodesian Lion Dog.

Although large, extremely powerful and bold the Ridgeback's gentlemanly nature can make it a superb family dog however, bouts of stubbornness and a difficulty to train tend to make it an unsuitable breed for the first–time owner.

Pastoral Dogs

The pastoral breeds come in all shapes and sizes from the diminutive Welsh Corgi through to the lightweight and agile Collies and the substantial German Shepherd Dogs to the heavyweight and hugely powerful Pyrenean Mountain Dog. Completely versatile, the Australian Kelpie will herd anything from cattle to poultry, the Komondor will protect sheep from raiding coyote, the Russian Samoyed is an expert at keeping reindeer in check – each

ONE OF THE MOST POPULAR CANINE groups, the Pastoral dog's heritage consists of many years spent working hard alongside farmers and shepherds herding and protecting livestock. Hardy in all respects, they would be expected to work amongst the roughest of terrain and in the harshest of weather.

has its own unique skills and techniques but all have played their part in defining the world as we know it today. Breeds that once acted as protectors of stock now excel as guardians of property. Others that used their alertness and intelligence to locate lost sheep became messengers and finders of wounded soldiers on the battlefields of Europe. Quick and eager to learn, they have since proven themselves to be masters of the agility ring and the obedience trial. They do, however, rely immensely on this high level of mental stimulation and without it can become stubborn and difficult to handle. As far as the pastoral breeds are concerned, a busy dog is a happy dog!

German Shepherd Dog (Alsatian)

German Shepherd Dog		
Breed Group	Pastoral	
Height	Bitch	55 – 60cm
	Male	60 – 65cm
Weight	Bitch	34 – 43kg
	Male	34 – 43kg
Lifespan	12 years	

ALMOST WOLF–LIKE IN APPEARance, the German Shepherd Dog, or GSD, has origins tracing back as far as the seventh century. Whilst originally bred for the herding of sheep and cattle it has, in more recent years, found extensive use as a guard and sniffer dog with the police and armed forces across the world.

It was fully established in the late nineteenth century by Rittmeister Max Emil Friedrich con Stephanitz, a German cavalry officer, and shown for the first time in 1882. Just seven years later an official club for the breed, the Verein für Deutsche Schäferhunde, was formed and began to undertake developing the GSD for military work. Impressed by its versatility and courage as both a messenger and a search and rescue dog with the German army, many allied soldiers took German

Fun Facts

A German Shepherd Dog called Rin–Tin–Tin was one of Hollywood's biggest stars of the 1920s and 30s. At the peak of his fame he would receive as many as 10,000 fan letters every week!

Shepherds home with them after the First World War although, due to anti–German sentiments, they were invariably known as Alsatians instead.

As a pet, a GSD will require a lot of time and patience and must be kept stimulated to prevent destructive ten-dencies showing through. They can enjoy and excel in obedience classes developing a strong social bond with their handler as they do so. Whilst gener-ally indifferent to children they will accept their presence happily as long as they are shown respect and not irritated.

Bearded Collie

IT IS THOUGHT THAT THE BEARDED Collie was first developed in Scotland during the eighteenth century from local sheepdog types including the Old English and, possibly, with an influx of international bloodlines from the Polish Lowland and Komondor breeds. Originally known as the Highland Collie, at one time it existed in two varieties – a lighter, more agile version used for herding upland flocks and a heavier type with a solid black coat that excelled at droving lowland cattle to market. It is thought that the contemporary Bearded Collie is a combination of these two.

It was first shown in the late 1800s but very nearly died out as a breed in the early twentieth century. It was thankfully revived just after the Second World War by Mrs G Olive Willison when she mated her bitch Jeannie to a dog called Bailie she had acquired from an emigrating gentleman she met on the beach! It is this bloodline that forms the basis of the modern day breed.

A Beardie, as the breed is usually known, makes for a superlative household pet. Enjoying all walks of family life, it revels in the chance to learn new skills and must, therefore, be kept men-

Bearded Collie		
Breed Group	Pastoral	
Height	Bitch	51 – 53cm
	Male	53 – 56cm
Weight	Bitch	18 – 28kg
	Male	18 – 28kg
Lifespan	16 – 17 years	

tally and physically active whenever possible. If allowed to get bored it will invariably entertain itself with an impromptu concert of wails and barks so it is inadvisable to leave a Bearded Collie alone for extended periods of time. With a long, flowing coat regular grooming is an absolute must.

Fun Facts

In 1989, Potterdale Classic of Moonhill owned by Mrs B White became the first and only Beardie to be crowned Best of Show at Crufts.

Border Collie

THE BORDER COLLIE IS THE CLASsic working farm dog and has gained favour across the world for its herding skills. Originating from the border country between England and Scotland, the breed has variously been known as the Working Collie, the Farm Collie and the English Collie. First mention was made as early as 1570 in the writings of Johannes Caius, physician to Queen Elizabeth I, in his Treatise on Englishe Dogges when he described the "shepherdes dogge" as "not huge, vaste, and bigge, but of an indifferent stature and growth" and commented on the fact that, whereas in France the sheep follow the shepherd "heere in our country the sheepherd followeth the sheepe!"

One Border Collie in particular is said to have had considerable influence on the modern breeds bloodline – Old Hemp, a tricolour dog born in 1893 with a quiet but powerful and commanding nature that sheep responded to with ease. He was used prodigiously as a stud dog and it is his working style that has been used successfully in sheepdog trials ever since.

No breed shows more willing to be trained than the Border Collie – its ability to absorb and understand new tasks

Border Collie		
Breed Group	Pastoral	
Height	Bitch	51 – 53cm
	Male	53 – 55cm
Weight	Bitch	14 – 17kg
	Male	17 – 20kg
Lifespan	12 – 14 years	

Fun Facts

The badge of the International Sheep Dog Society portrays a Border Collie in its herding pose. The dog featured was Wiston Cap – the most popular and used stud dog in the breed's long history.

with ease making it the ideal candidate for trials, agility, obedience and even fly-ball. Unsurprisingly, they demand a considerable amount of exercise – in excess of two hours is required on a daily basis. Bright, lively and alert, they make good pets especially with families where they can exhibit their herding tendencies on errant children.

Briard

Briard		
Breed Group	Pastoral	
Height	Bitch	56 – 64cm
	Male	62 – 68cm
Weight	Bitch	34kg
	Male	38kg
Lifespan	10 – 12 years	

OFTEN DESCRIBED AS "A STRONG and gentle heart wrapped in fur", the Briard's most distant ancestry remains a bit of an enigma although it is commonly thought it was first established in Europe during the Middle Ages after the crossing of eastern sheepherding dogs and indigenous guarding breeds.

Two theories exist as to the origins of its name. The first is quite simple in that it is derived from the Parisian environ of Brie. The second is far more romantic and involves the untimely murder in 1371 of French nobleman Sir Aubry de Montdidier in the forest of Bondy. It is said that after his death Aubry's dog, Dragon, relentlessly pursued a man called Richard of Macaire. With suspicions raised Richard was condemned by the King to a judiciary duel with the dog. Dragon killed Macaire who, in his dying breath, confessed to the murder of the dog's master. It is said that chien d'Aubry, dog of Aubry, may have over time become chien d'brie.

Away from their herding duties, Briards have a long and esteemed military record having accompanied Napoleon Bonaparte on his military

campaigns and then, as the official dog of the French army, been utilised extensively in the First World War to carry messages, ammunition and medical supplies to the front line and to find wounded soldiers.

Big and strong the Briard is a naturally protective creature and, with a particular love of children, makes for a good family dog. It loves to play games when given the opportunity although these can often turn quite rough therefore care should be taken with particularly young children in a household.

Fun Facts

Despite its ancient origins the Briard was only introduced to the United Kingdom in 1966 when a dog arrived from Ireland. The first litter was born in England three years later in 1969.

Rough Collie

Rough Collie		
Breed Group	Pastoral	
Height	Bitch	51 – 56cm
	Male	56 – 61cm
Weight	Bitch	23 – 30kg
	Male	27 – 34kg
Lifespan	12 – 14 years	

IT IS PROBABLE THAT THE ROUGH Collie owes its existence to the hardy dogs that accompanied the Roman invaders of Britain and a variety of native Scottish breeds. Known for many years simply as the Scottish Sheepdog, its common name is most likely to have been taken from a type of black sheep known as a Colley. Its popularity is largely due to the attentions of Queen Victoria who, whilst visiting her beloved Balmoral estate in the 1860s, became enamoured with its beauty and took some back home with her to Windsor Castle.

With this royal endorsement it quickly established itself as a desirable showing dog and soon also found favour across the Atlantic in the United States. It is there that the Rough Collie found yet more fame – this time as

Fun Facts

Although the character of Lassie is female, all of the animals to play her in the original films were male! This was because the female Rough Collie loses its coat at least once a year making it unsuitable for year-round filming.

part of Hollywood's burgeoning movie industry with the release of the film Lassie Come Home based upon the novel by British–American author Eric Knight.

Intelligent and friendly, Rough Collies make exceptional, loving family pets and are particularly fond of children. Considering their breeding, they require relatively little exercise (60–80 minutes per day) as long as they are given the opportunity to spend at least some of this time off the lead and running free. Time saved walking is, however, likely to be time spent grooming as their silky, long double coat requires frequent brushing to prevent matting.

Contrary to popular belief they do not possess a natural ability to save lost children from wells or abandoned mines.

Old English Sheepdog

Old English Sheepdog		
Breed Group	Pastoral	
Height	Bitch	56 – 66cm
	Male	61 – 71cm
Weight	Bitch	30 – 40kg
	Male	36 – 46kg
Lifespan	12 – 13 years	

THE OLD ENGLISH SHEEPDOG emerged in the West Country during the mid eighteenth century where it was developed as a sheep herding and cattle droving dog. Its ancestry is a subject up for debate but it is thought to contain genes from the Bearded Collie, the Bergamasco, the Briard and the Armant. By exhibiting great intelligence and a surprising level of agility, its reputation quickly spread and the Old English Sheepdog soon gained favour with agricultural communities across the land.

Old English Sheepdogs traditionally have their tails docked at the first joint – a fact which has earned it the nickname of Bobtail (or just plain Bob).

Fun Facts

In the eighteenth century dogs were not groomed as they are today so the Old English Sheepdog would find itself being sheered alongside the sheep it herded and protected.
Farmer's wives would then spin the dog's shorn coat with sheeps wool to make warm and water resistant clothing.

This practice harks back to the days when a tax exemption was granted on dogs that were used for droving – these animals were marked by having their tails removed.

Immensely faithful, friendly and rather extrovert, the Old English Sheepdog makes a good family pet but can be excitable and shows a tendency for rough play. Although loving in nature and big in heart it is, nevertheless, a fearless creature and can display a fierce, window rattling bark if it suspects the presence of an intruder.

Pyrenean Mountain Dog

Pyrenean Mountain Dog		
Breed Group	Pastoral	
Height	Bitch	65 – 72cm
	Male	70 – 80cm
Weight	Bitch	40 – 55kg
	Male	50 – 60kg
Lifespan	11 – 12 years	

UNSURPRISINGLY, THE PYRENEAN Mountain Dog heralds from the border region between France and Spain. One of the most physically powerful breeds ever created, it was used for many years to protect upland flocks of sheep from the ravages of attacking wolves and brown bears. Known as the Great Pyrenees in the United States, its true origins remain unclear but it is generally thought to be a distant relative of Tibetan Mastiffs brought from Asia in the Middle Ages by nomadic tribesmen with additional influences from the Hungarian Kuvasz and the Italian Maremma – all of which bear a striking resemblance.

Having already established a reputation in the thirteenth century as a fearsome guard dog protecting the chateaux of Lourdes and Foix, the Pyr gained royal approval in 1675 after the French Dauphin, the 8–year–old son of Louis XIV, visited Barèges and befriended one named Patou. On leaving he insisted that the dog should return to live with him in Paris at the Louvre. In its honour, the King bestowed the Pyrenean Mountain Dog with the title Royal Dog of France.

Popularity of the breed declined after the French Revolution and the breed became scarce however, in the early twentieth century the work of Bernard Sénac–Lagrange ensured its survival.

Selective breeding has now ensured the Pyr is gentle and kind in nature. Whilst clearly unsuitable for the novice dog owner, they are obedient, loyal and intelligent and mix well with children and other household pets – as such, they make a good addition to any family providing they possess a considerable surplus of living space.

Fun Facts

Pyrenean Mountain Dogs were once used to smuggle contraband over the French–Spanish border as their strength, agility and sure-footedness allowed them to use mountain passes inaccessible to customs officials.

Terriers

TERRIERS ARE HUNTING DOGS AT heart – bred and refined over many years to tackle all manner of vermin and burrowing animals from foxes and badgers to rabbits and rats. Largely a British creation, their name harks back to the first century and the Roman invasion. Seeing these hardy and tenacious little creatures at work over and under the ground they named them terrarii, from the Latin term terra, meaning earth.

Over the many years they have worked the countryside, terriers have become real specialists in their various arts. Some, like the Fox Terrier, Bedlington and Jack Russell were developed with speed and stamina to match the pace of a hunt in full flight whilst others, such as the Airedale, are more at home in the water. Others celebrate a less salubrious past having been created solely as canine fighting machines for use in the bear and dog pits prior to the passing of the Cruelty to Animals Act in 1835.

Quick witted and alert, rugged, single–minded and independent the terrier is as popular today as it ever has been having made a superb transition from working dog to household pet.

Border Terrier

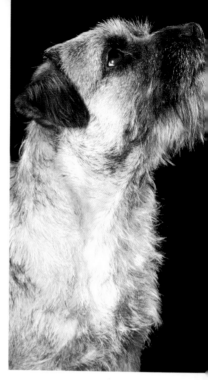

Border Terrier		
Breed Group	Terrier	
Height	Bitch	28cm
	Male	31cm
Weight	Bitch	5 – 7kg
	Male	6 – 7kg
Lifespan	15 years +	

ALSO KNOWN IN THE PAST AS the Reedwater Terrier or the Coquetdale Terrier, the Border Terrier has changed little since it first appeared in the nineteenth century. It was, and still is, used as a working terrier on the border country between England and Scotland where its naturally rugged stature and wiry dense coat proved ideal for coping

Fun Facts

In the 1985 Walt Disney film Return to Oz, Dorothy's pet dog Toto was played by a Border Terrier called Tansy. (In the 1939 original, The Wizard of Oz, a Cairn Terrier by the name of Terry played the same role).

with rough and remote moorland and fells on cold, wet days in the company of a hunt. Although far from being unattractive, the Border Terrier was never bred for its good looks but rather for its ability to match a horse for speed in open country and still follow a fox to ground to end a pursuit. Strong of jaw and long in leg it has, for many years, shown that it is more than a match for the task.

Brave, fun loving and affectionate the Border Terrier makes for an exceptional family pet and is especially good around children of all ages. Whilst intelligent and immensely trainable, they do, however, invariably retain a strongly independent streak that requires both patience and a firm hand.

They are very active and demand a high level of exercise on a daily basis and are likely to chase any small creature with complete disregard for their own wellbeing or safety but will happily live in harmony with household pets if introduced to them at a young age.

Bull Terrier

IN THE DARKER DAYS OF EIGHT-eenth century England, Old English Bulldogs were crossbred with tenacious terrier types to produce the "Bull and Terrier" – a ferocious creature trained to fight to the death in a pit against similarly bred dogs and even larger animals. Later, Whippet strains were included to increase the breed's speed and agility before Irish born Birmingham dog dealer James Hinks all but defined the breed we known today by introducing bloodlines from the English White Terrier in the early 1860s. This refined breed displayed the long, smooth head, short powerful legs and small, erect ears of the type as we know it today. Hinks celebrated his creation by naming it the Bull Terrier.

In recent years and through little fault of its own, the Bull Terrier has become a much maligned breed and has often been

Bull Terrier		
Breed Group	Terrier	
Height	Bitch	45cm
	Male	45cm
Weight	Bitch	33kg
	Male	33kg
Lifespan	10 – 12 years	

Fun Facts

In Charles Dickens' Oliver Twist, the villainous Bill Sikes is the owner of a white Bull Terrier called Bullseye who is his ultimate undoing when he leads the police to Fagin's lair.

regarded by sensationalist media as a dangerous breed – the reality, however, is somewhat different. Whilst their immense physical strength and occasionally obstinate behaviour makes them unsuitable for the novice owner, they possess a naturally placid demeanour, are wonderfully friendly and playful and have a delightful, cheeky sense of humour. They are very affectionate, especially gentle with children and enjoy company – in all an ideal family pet!

Staffordshire Bull Terrier

KNOWN AFFECTIONATELY AS THE Staffie, the Staffordshire Bull Terrier emerged in the seventeenth century as one of the Bull and Terrier fighting breeds. As bull–baiting slipped into decline there became a need to develop a new breed more suited to the burgeoning sport of dog–fighting.

These dogs although full of tenacity and utterly ferocious in combat, were renowned for their courage, affectionate nature and, incredibly, the fact that they made excellent and loving companions and guardians for children – as such they were handsomely patronised by the rich aristocracy and the poor working man alike. When the introduction of the Humane Act in 1835 put an end to the barbarity of dog–fighting, a group of enthusiasts from Staffordshire decided to help preserve the breed by naming it the Staffordshire Bull Terrier and by setting a standard for its impressive physical attributes.

The Staffie was officially recognised by the Kennel Club in 1935 and has since risen to great popularity in the United Kingdom where they continue to prove themselves to be an ideal canine companion – so much so that they are currently the fifth most popular canine breed registered. Full of energy, they require a considerable amount of daily exercise – at least two hours per day – if their boisterousness is to be kept properly in check. They are bright, intelligent, obedient and, above all, very loving.

Staffordshire Bull Terrier		
Breed Group	Terrier	
Height	Bitch	35.5 – 40.5cm
	Male	35.5 – 40.5cm
Weight	Bitch	11 – 15.5kg
	Male	12.7 – 17kg
Lifespan	12 – 14 years	

West Highland White Terrier

West Highland White Terrier		
Breed Group	Terrier	
Height	Bitch	25 – 28cm
	Male	25 – 28cm
Weight	Bitch	7 – 10kg
	Male	7 – 10kg
Lifespan	13 – 14 years	

WEST HIGHLAND WHITE TERRIERS, or Westies for short, were originally bred to hunt foxes, otters, rats and other vermin and share their distant ancestry with the Cairn Terrier, Dandie Dinmont and, of course, the Scottish Terrier. It is said that, after accidentally shooting his favourite dark–coloured terrier whilst hunting on his Argyllshire estate, Colonel Edward Malcolm of Poltalloch vowed only to own white dogs thereafter. Through selective breeding the ancestor of the Westie was born although at this time it was known as the Poltalloch Terrier. Later in the nineteenth century the name was changed to the Rose–neath Terrier in honour of the Dumbartonshire estate of George Campbell, 8th Duke of Argyll, who

Fun Facts

Written and illustrated by the great Cecil Aldin in 1912, Mac – A Story of a Dog tells the tale of a West Highland White Terrier considered a "braw and canny Scot" just eight years after the breed was formally recognised.

favoured and patronised the breed. Finally, in 1904, they became known as the West Highland White Terrier.

The Westie is invariably seen as a bright, confident, affectionate and, above all, cheeky character. It is exceptionally loyal and loves playing with young children – luckily for the West Highland White, it's a somewhat robust breed! They require a good, but not excessive, level of exercise – ball games and chasing cats being particular favourites.

Airedale Terrier

THE LARGEST OF THE TERRIER group, the Airedale was first bred to hunt otters and large rats. It was developed in the nineteenth century in Airedale and Wharfedale in the heart of the Yorkshire dales by hunters, crossing the now extinct Black and Tan Terrier with the Otterhound and then later introducing additional bloodlines from the Irish and Welsh Terriers. The result was a big, strong and resilient breed that boasted a stiff, wiry, protective coat and displayed remarkable skill as an expert and agile swimmer.

The advent of the twentieth century took the Airedale Terrier's repertoire into new territories. Following training from Edwin Hautenville Richardson, a number of the breed were brought into service with local constabularies as service dogs. The animals proved to be a resounding success and with the advent of the First World War Hautenville Richardson wasted no time in convincing the British Army that they too could benefit from the Airedale's unique skills. Assigned the rank of Colonel, he established the War Dog Training School at Shoeburyness in Essex and set about preparing terriers as guard dogs and messengers. One such Airedale, a

dog called Jack, was posthumously awarded a Victoria Cross after fighting his way through bombs, bullets and half a mile of thick mud with a broken jaw and a shattered front leg to deliver a message. His actions saved an entire battalion of soldiers.

These days the Airedale Terrier is treated to a far more sedate lifestyle. Friendly, loyal and loving they make excellent family dogs and show a particular affinity with children. With an alert mind and a fierce bark they make worthy guardians of house and home but are not generally aggressive to other dogs. Intelligent and amenable to training they can also excel in obedience and agility classes.

Airedale Terrier

Breed Group	Terrier	
Height	Bitch	56 – 59cm
	Male	58 – 61cm
Weight	Bitch	22kg
	Male	22kg
Lifespan	12 – 15 years	

Bedlington Terrier

Bedlington Terrier		
Breed Group	Terrier	
Height	Bitch	38 – 43cm
	Male	38 – 43cm
Weight	Bitch	8 – 10kg
	Male	8 – 10kg
Lifespan	12 – 16 years	

THEY SAY THAT APPEARANCES can be deceiving and this is never truer than when dealing with the Bedlington Terrier. Long of leg and lean in body it can look more like a young lamb than a dog but this really is a wolf in sheep's clothing – albeit a diminutive one!

First named the Rothbury Terrier after the Northumberland coalmining community it originally possessed a much heavier body and shorter legs. However, cross breeding with the Whippet and the Dandie Dinmont in the late eighteenth and possibly the early nineteenth centuries saw it transformed into a faster, finer breed. Fierce and relentless in a fight, swift of foot and blessed with an acute sense of smell it was an excellent hunter and soon

became a favourite sidekick of poachers earning it the nickname of the Gypsy Dog. The breed is not the easiest to deal with but time, patience and perseverance will reward an owner with a loving, affectionate and loyal house pet. They need to be trained early in life to socialise with other pets and time should also be taken to introduce the young pup to other dogs whether part of the family unit or not. An effective guard dog, strangers will be clearly announced although welcome guests will soon be greeted in a friendly and enthusiastic manner.

Fun Facts

The earliest recorded ancestor of the Bedlington Terrier was a dog called Old Flint who was whelped in 1792.

Jack Russell Terrier

Jack Russell Terrier		
Breed Group	Terrier	
Height	Bitch	25 – 35cm
	Male	35 – 33cm
Weight	Bitch	5 – 8kg
	Male	5 – 8kg
Lifespan	9 – 15 years	

ONE OF THE MOST POPULAR BREEDS of all time, the humble Jack Russell Terrier for many years struggled to gain the recognition it rightfully deserved. Shunned by international kennel clubs for decades, it is only now becoming seen as an official breed type.

The Reverend John "Jack" Russell, known as the Sporting Parson, is credited with having established the breed after he purchased a little white terrier bitch whilst walking in Oxford. Named Trump, she formed the base for a breeding program that set out to develop a small terrier with sufficient speed and stamina to take pace with the hunt but that was small and courageous enough to chase a fox that had gone to ground. After the Reverend's death his dogs were taken on by other hunting enthusiasts and the breed started to flourish.

As sporting dogs became less in

demand, working Jack Russells often found themselves being taken on as household pets – a role they pursue with great relish. Happy, enthusiastic and deeply loyal they fit well into family life. Highly intelligent, fun loving and always eager to learn they can excel in pastimes such as dog agility trials and flyball.

With character and ability always prized high over physical appearance, the modern day Jack Russell can vary considerably. There are short and long legged varieties as well as smooth and rough coated. All, however, offer a cheerful smile and a spring in their step.

Toy Dogs

THE TOY BREEDS HAVE ONE OF THE most important jobs in the world of dogs – to act as the perfect companion. The name Toy refers not to playability but to size – the term simply refers to the various breeds' diminutive stature. Prizing form over ability, nearly all have been specifi-cally bred for a pleasing appearance and a quiet demeanour.

Although the breeds have only been referred to as Toy dogs since the middle of the nineteenth century they have existed for thousands of years. It is known that the ancient Chinese revered their Lion Dogs as sacred whilst Romans doted on their lapdogs. In medieval times they found favour as footwarmers and to French courtiers they were a statement of fashion.

Where these animals once graced the houses of nobility and the royal courts of Europe and Asia they now play an essential role in the lives and wellbeing of thousands of people including the elderly, the housebound and the ill. There role has, perhaps, never been so important.

Yorkshire Terrier

Yorkshire Terrier		
Breed Group	Terrier	
Height	Bitch	18 – 20cm
	Male	18 – 20cm
Weight	Bitch	2 – 3kg
	Male	2 – 3kg
Lifespan	9 – 15 years	

ALTHOUGH A TERRIER BY NAME, the Yorkie, as it is commonly known, is classed as one of the Toy group of dogs. Compared with many traditional breeds it is a quite recent phenomenon and considered to be wholly man–made. During a period of immigration from Scotland to the Pennine mill towns of Lancashire and Yorkshire in the 1850s, it is thought that weavers brought with them a hardy local breed called the Scotch or Halifax Terrier. This interbred with small, local terrier breeds including the Manchester Terrier and the Dandie Dinmont.

Considered for many years as a breed of the working classes it earned its keep as an expert ratter working in the mills and mines that peppered the landscape.

Fun Facts

A match–box sized Yorkie by the name of Sylvia holds the record as the smallest dog in recorded history. Owned by Arthur Maples of Blackburn she stood just over 6cm to the shoulder, was less than 9cm from nose to tail and weighed in at about 110 grams – that's about the same as an iPod!

It is often said that Yorkies were also bred to protect children from rat–bites at night with one on guard at the head of the bed and another at the foot.

The fact that the Yorkshire Terrier is one of the smallest of breeds seems to have escaped no–one but the Yorkie itself for it is more than prepared to take on the largest and ferocious breeds with scant regard for its own safety or wellbeing. They are, however, a loving and loyal breed that likes nothing better than to curl up on a warm lap on a cold winters evening.

Pug

TAKING ITS NAME FROM THE OLD English word pugg, a jovial term for a playful little devil or monkey, there are two theories as to the origins of this wrinkly little breed. The first is that it was a miniature version of a somewhat rare French mastiff known as the Dogue de Bordeaux. The second and more widely recognised explanation is that it was first bred in the east of China during the Shang Dynasty. Known as the Lo–Chiang–Sze or Foo, it was a prized possession of Chinese ruling classes and was often kept in great luxury sometimes with an armed guard of its own.

In the late sixteenth century, Dutch traders subsequently brought the Pug to Europe where it gained instant favour and was declared the official dog of the House of Orange, the Royal Family of the Netherlands.

Pug		
Breed Group	Toy	
Height	Bitch	30 – 36cm
	Male	30 – 36cm
Weight	Bitch	6 – 8kg
	Male	6 – 8kg
Lifespan	10 – 15 years	

Fun Facts

Artist William Hogarth (1697–1764) owned a Pug called Trump who appeared in a number of his works including a self portrait titled The Painter and his Pug which is now displayed in the Tate Gallery, London.

Their popularity spread quickly and soon no self respecting, well heeled member of the aristocracy could be seen without one. William III, Marie Antoinette, Goya and Hogarth all became owners of Pugs over the centuries – Queen Victoria herself was a keen exponent of the breed.

Self–confident, playful and with an endearingly mischievous nature, the Pug's character belies its regal past. It is, however, intelligent, attentive and loyal and is always willing to please its owner. It does not bark excessively but is always alert and makes a good pocket–sized watch dog.

Cavalier King Charles Spaniel

THE CAVALIER KING CHARLES Spaniel is often regarded as the most Royal of all dogs having been shown great favour by both Mary Queen of Scots and Charles II of England. In fact, it was Charles himself who bestowed it with the honour of his own name.

It is thought that the breed originated from either China or Japan before finally reaching England from France in the sixteenth century. Used for many years on shoots as a cocker,

CAVALIER KING CHARLES SPANIEL

the King Charles Spaniel of old had a flat head, high set ears and a pointed nose but was gradually changed through selective breeding to produce the shorter nosed animal we recognise today. At the height of its popularity in Victorian times the King Charles Spaniel was known as a comforte dog such was its reputation as an admirable companion to young and old – doctors were even known to prescribe them as a remedy.

Gentle and undemanding they are an easy dog to own and train and given affection will offer much in return. They socialise well with cats and other family pets and can be trusted with children. Happy to remain quietly curled up on a friendly lap they are an ideal companion for the elderly or infirm.

Cavalier King Charles Spaniel		
Breed Group	Toy	
Height	Bitch	30 – 33cm
	Male	30 – 33cm
Weight	Bitch	5 – 8kg
	Male	5 – 8kg
Lifespan	13 – 15 years	

Bichon Frise

Bichon Frise		
Breed Group	Toy	
Height	Bitch	25 – 30cm
	Male	25 – 30cm
Weight	Bitch	3 – 6kg
	Male	3 – 6kg
Lifespan	15 – 17 years	

THE HISTORY OF THE BICHON Frise is as extravagant and extraordinary as the breed itself. Although it is often thought of as a French breed, it is known that Bichon type dogs were developed many centuries ago on the islands of the Mediterranean and in the Canaries. Tenerife is thought to be the original home of the Bichon Frise from where it was brought by Italian and Spanish sailors to mainland Europe during the fourteenth century. With a toy–like appearance it gained favour with the noble families of France but fell from grace in the wake of the revolution.

Bright, agile and easily taught, the Bichon then found fame as a circus

Fun Facts

Originally the Bichon breeds were divided into four types the Bichon Bolognaise that lived in and around Bologna, and the Bichon Tenerife, the Bichon Maltais, and the Bichon Havanais. The name Bichon a Pool Frise which became shortened to just Bichon Frise was only introduced in 1933.

performer – earning its keep as a canine clown and organ grinder – but over the decades the breed's numbers still gradually declined. The advent of the First World War appeared to do little to help however, many servicemen took a liking to its plucky nature and after hostilities ceased breeders once again took notice of them.

Translated, Bichon Frise simply means "curly lapdog" – a highly appropriate name considering this breed's happy and loving demeanour. Ideal as a child's pet they love to take part in family activities but are also equally content being left alone occasionally.

Chihuahua

Chihuahua		
Breed Group	Toy	
Height	Bitch	15 – 23cm
	Male	15 – 23cm
Weight	Bitch	1 – 2.7kg
	Male	1 – 2.7kg
Lifespan	15 – 20 years +	

ONE OF THE SMALLEST BREEDS, the tiny Chihuahua has had a colourful past. Its exact origins remain a mystery but it is known that carvings of small Chihuahua like dogs adorned the fifth century Mayan pyramids of Chichen Itza on what is now Mexico's Yucatan Peninsular and that images similar to these have also been found in the ninth century Toltec stones used to build the monastery of Huejotzingo in Puebla.

Champion Bramerita Naughty But Nice, Doughnut to her friends, is a British born Chihuahua bitch and the most successful show dog of any breed in history. She has won over 100 challenge certificates and championships at home and abroad including seven consecutive wins at Crufts.

It is understood that a small dog known as a Techichi was considered an important part of the Aztec and Toltec cultures. They were kept by the wealthy and performed a key role in religious practices of the time. Unfortunately for the poor Techichi, its most important role came after the demise of its master when it would be cremated with the deceased in order to take on its sins and act as a spirit guide through the underworld.

The Chihuahua itself is thought to have been bred by crossing the ancient Techichi with other small dogs from Mexico, Arizona and Texas and is named after the Mexican state where it was discovered in 1850. It was first exported to the United States in 1898.

Although completely unintimidated by other dogs regardless of size or breed it remains fussy about the human company it keeps but will invariably form a strong bond with its master or mistress. Chihuahuas are easy to manage and require little exercise but are highly territorial and, equipped with a shrill voice that likes to be heard, are not the obvious choice for those looking for a quiet life.

Chinese Crested

Chinese Crested		
Breed Group	Toy	
Height	Bitch	23 – 33cm
	Male	23 – 33cm
Weight	Bitch	4 – 5kg
	Male	4 – 5kg
Lifespan	12 – 15 years	

IF EVER THERE WAS A UNIQUE looking dog it is the Chinese Crested. Two varieties of the breed exist – the Hairless and the Powderpuff – but incredibly, with the hairlessness being a regressive condition, both types can be born to a single litter. Just to confuse matters, it is possible for a Hairless Chinese Crested to actually have some hair! This, however, would be in the form of a light and perhaps incomplete single coat whilst the Powderpuff boasts a rich, thick double coat.

Although its name gives a clue to an Oriental past, the breed is thought to have actually originated in southern Africa from where Chinese merchants took examples back home on board trading ships. Renamed the Chinese Crested, it arrived in Europe in the late nineteenth century but has always been met with a mixed reception – some

Fun Facts

The most famous Chinese Crested was perhaps Sam. With extremely wrinkled hairless skin, deformed teeth and cataracts in his eyes he was voted the World's Ugliest Dog in a 2005 competition.

people understandably finding the idea of a bald canine a little too unusual for their taste.

Chinese Crested's are usually very affectionate and enjoy spending at least some of their time as a lap dog. They do, however, enjoy bouts of energetic play and have been known to do extremely well in dog agility trials where they get the chance to put their considerable intelligence to good use. Although it remains a superb, if unusual, family pet, care must be taken in hot weather to protect its sensitive skin from the rays of the sun. A Chinese Crested can get sunburn just like me and you!

Papillon

THE PAPILLON BREED IS THOUGHT to date back over 700 years but little is known of its history prior to 1545. It is suspected that the Dwarf Spaniel is the natural ancestor of the breed and that it most probably originated in the Orient before becoming refined in France and Belgium. The older variety of the breed was known as the Phalène – French for night moth – because its dropped ears were carried in the same way that a moth folds its wings. Like so many of the ostentatious toy breeds, it quickly gained favour with the nobility of France and Spain and it is written that Marie Antoinette took her beloved Phalène with her to the guillotine.

The type, as we recognise it, was developed in the late nineteenth century by Belgian and French breeders and first shown in Britain in 1923. With erect, fringed ears it was given the name

Papillon		
Breed Group	Toy	
Height	Bitch	20 – 28cm
	Male	20 – 28cm
Weight	Bitch	1.8 – 4kg
	Male	1.8 – 4kg
Lifespan	12 – 15 years	

Fun Facts

After her death, Marie Antoinette's dogs were taken from the scaffold and lovingly cared for. The house in which they stayed still exists in the centre of Paris – it is called Papillon House.

Papillon – French for butterfly. It is sometimes also known as a Chien Écureuil, or squirrel dog, in reference to the plumed tail it carries so elegantly.

The Papillon is intelligent and friendly, is easy to train and shows little aggression to other dogs to a point of indifference. It requires relatively little exercise and loves human company and lots of attention – especially when it is given the opportunity to get involved with family activities.

Pekingese

Pekingese		
Breed Group	Toy	
Height	Bitch	15 – 23cm
	Male	15 – 23cm
Weight	Bitch	5.5kg
	Male	5.5kg
Lifespan	13 – 15 years	

IF LEGENDS ARE TO BE BELIEVED, the Pekingese is the result of a deal with Buddha. It is said that a mighty lion and a marmoset fell in love but that the lion was too large. The lion went to see Buddha and was told that he could marry the marmoset but would have to sacrifice his size and his strength. The lion agreed and the result was the dog we know as the Pekingese.

Because of this, the Chinese considered the Pekingese, or Lion Dog, to be a divine creature. Common people had to bow to them, were forbidden to own them and to steal one was a crime punished by death by stoning. The breed finally reached the outside world in 1860 after British and French soldiers overran the Summer Palace at the height of the Second Opium War. Guards had been ordered to kill the

Fun Facts

A Pekingese was one of only two dogs to survive the sinking of the RMS Titanic in 1913. Named Sun Yat Sen after a Chinese statesman it was the property of Henry Sleeper Harper of the Harper Brothers publishing company.

dogs to prevent them falling into enemy hands but five were found and "liberated". Of these, a pair was given to the Duchess of Richmond and another pair was taken by Lord Hay.

The fifth was presented to the nation's principal dog lover of the day – Queen Victoria herself. It is these few dogs that formed the basis of the breed as we know it today.

Living up to their leonine heritage, the Pekingese is generally found to be regal and dignified, however, they do possess a mischievous streak that can sometimes manifest itself at the most unlikely of moments. They show little aggression and make ideal family pets requiring as little as 20 minutes exercise per day although the time saved is likely to be spent grooming its very long coat.

Utility Dogs

diverse selection of breeds has become ever more popular. Such is the group's diversity, different national Kennel Clubs have trouble in agreeing which dogs should or shouldn't appear in it.

The group contains some of the most curious, distinctive and unusual of all the breeds from the patriotic British Bulldog to the wrinkly Chinese Shar Pei

THE UTILITY DOG GROUP IS THE most curious of all. Officially the term refers to being fit for purpose but the reality is that it is the canine equivalent of a big box file labelled miscellaneous and in recent years its stunningly

and from the enlightened Tibetan Lhasa Apso to the majestic Japanese Akita. They have held the most extraordinary occupations – some were employed to deter highwaymen, others acted as a nineteenth century form of fire–truck siren, some were sacred others were symbols of national pride but all have now earned their place in the hearts of dog lovers everywhere.

Shih Tzu

Shih Tzu		
Breed Group	Utility	
Height	Bitch	23 – 27cm
	Male	26 – 27cm
Weight	Bitch	4 –8kg
	Male	4 – 8kg
Lifespan	15 – 18 years	

THOUGH THE SHIH TZU IS CLASSED and widely regarded as a Chinese breed its true heritage can be traced back much further to the sacred Lion Dog of Tibet – a breed we now know as the Lhasa Apso. These were often given as gifts to the Manchu emperors of China by the Dalai Lama and it is thought that interbreeding with the Pekingese and possibly the Chinese Pug by the Dowager Empress Tzu Hsi led to the creation of the Shih Tzu breed – its name meaning Little Lion in Mandarin.

In the pre–war years, several Shih Tzus were brought to Europe, a pair of which ended up in England having been acquired by Lady Brownrigg, the wife of the Quarter Master General to the North China Command. Her black and white dog and bitch, named Hibou and Shu–ssa, along with another dog,

Lung–fu–ssa, which was brought to Ireland, form the bloodline of many Shih Tzus in existence today.

Short and muscular, the Shih Tzu is affectionate, playful and energetic in character. It is wary of strangers and, as such, makes a superb watchdog. Due to issues with eye infections its long crown–hair is usually tied up in a samurai like top–knot.

Schnauzer

ORIGINATING FROM THE LIVE-stock farming areas of Württemberg and Bavaria in the southwest of Germany, a recognisable Schnauzer type of dog can be seen in works of art dating from as early as the late fifteenth century. These early dogs were excellent general purpose animals with a reputation as an adept rat–catcher, capable hunter, workmanlike drover and formi-

dable guard dog – their natural disposition leading them to be vocal rather than aggressive to strangers.

For many years the breed was called simply the Wire–Haired Pinscher but after a handsome dog by the name of Schnauze – a name derived from the German for snout – won its class at the prestigious Hanover International show in 1879 the name was changed. It is cur-

rently the only dog breed in existence that is named after one of its own.

Schnauzers are bred in three distinct varieties – the Standard, the Miniature and the Giant. The smallest of these is the result of crossing the Standard with the Affenpinscher and other small breeds and was used exclusively as a ratter. The largest, by contrast, earned its keep originally as a cattle drover but is now more often seen in police and security work.

Affable, alert and energetic they make fine family pets requiring a reasonable but not excessive level of daily exercise. They are good with children and other household pets if introduced at a young age.

Schnauzer		
Breed Group	Utility	
Height	Bitch	43 – 48cm
	Male	46 – 51cm
Weight	Bitch	16kg
	Male	18kg
Lifespan	12 – 17 years	

Lhasa Apso

WITH ORIGINS HARKING BACK TO the ancient Buddhist temples of Tibet, the Lhasa Apso's wise and sage–like appearance seems curiously appropriate. Rarely seen out of its native land, its precise roots remain unclear but legend tells how Manjusri, the bodhisattva or god of wisdom and awareness, was usually accompanied by a small dog that could transform itself into a mighty lion. With its obvious leonine looks, the Lhasa Apso was often associated with this deity. For many years it was considered sacred and remained the property of monks and holy men – when the master died it was thought that his spirit would enter the body of his dog.

The first Lhasa Apso's to venture outside of Tibet were gifts presented to the Manchu emperors of China by the Dalai Lama. This tradition soon spread to other visiting dignitaries and finally, in the early twentieth century, the Lhasa reached British shores. As you would expect for a breed that has spent the last two millennia absorbing the worldly and enlightened souls of Tibet's greatest holy men, the Lhasa Apso is a loyal, intelligent and trusting breed. It makes an excellent pet and is particularly good with children. As you would expect from an animal like this, its coat requires thorough grooming on a regular basis to avoid matting.

Lhaso Apso		
Breed Group	Utility	
Height	Bitch	23 – 25cm
	Male	25 – 28cm
Weight	Bitch	5 – 6kg
	Male	6 – 7kg
Lifespan	17 – 18 years	

Fun Facts

Before being brought to the West, the Lhasa Apso dogs lived a vegetarian existence in line with the Tibetan Buddhist teaching that killing was not permissible – even fleas were picked off by hand and placed in a jar before being carried away into a valley and released back to the wild.

Bulldog

Bulldog		
Breed Group	Utility	
Height	Bitch	31 – 36cm
	Male	31 – 36cm
Weight	Bitch	23 – 25kg
	Male	23 – 25kg
Lifespan	8 years	

FOR MANY THE ARCHETYPAL symbol of everything British, the Bulldog can trace its ancestry back to pre–Christian times. It is thought that they are derived from the extinct Bullenbeisser – a powerful mastiff–like dog with Middle Eastern origins that were used as guardians and for slaying wild animals. Probably brought to England by Phoenician traders in the sixth century BC it was bred into a smaller, more practical dog during the reign of King John in the thirteenth century for the purpose of bull–baiting – a barbaric blood–sport that saw the dogs pitted against an angry staked bull.

The Bulldog was ideal for the job – almost impervious to pain, its heavy

Fun Facts

One of the most famous living Bulldogs is Darla. She lives in Pasadena California and likes to eat and lounge about like other dogs. But she also has another special pastime to while away the hours – skateboarding! She can do tricks and stunts and even has her own website!

head and shoulders made it less likely to have its back broken in the melee whilst its strong, locking jaw made it near impossible to shake off. The introduction in 1835 of the Cruelty to Animals Act outlawed this so–called sport but, fortunately, the popular Bulldog breed was preserved.

Time and careful breeding has seen it transformed into the most wonderful of household pets with a temperament unmatched by any other type of dog. Although rather stubborn and relatively difficult to train, Bulldogs invariably adore young children and, with a comical nature, children invariably love them. They require very little exercise and generally would rather be curled up on a sofa than trudging mile after mile across hill and dale.

Akita

Akita		
Breed Group	Utility	
Height	Bitch	61 – 66cm
	Male	66 – 71cm
Weight	Bitch	34 – 50kg
	Male	34 – 50kg
Lifespan	15 years +	

A MEMBER OF THE SPITZ FAMILY, the Akita is the largest of the Japanese breeds and was originally bred in the seventeenth century in the province on Honshu Island with which it shares its name. Used extensively by the police in modern times, the breed has remained unchanged for many centuries after having been created as a fighter and as a hunter of black bear, wild boar and deer.

In the late nineteenth century the native Japanese breeds all suffered in popularity due to the importation of Western breeds such as the German Shepherd and the Pointer. However, the breed was preserved following the formation of the Society for the Preservation of Japanese Dogs who

Fun Facts

In the Tokyo Shibuya railway station there stands a statue of Chuken Hachi–ko, Loyal Dog Hachi – an Akita who faithfully greeted his master at the station each day on his return from work. This devoted animal journeyed to the station daily for 10 years after his master died.

declared that all indigenous breeds were national monuments. Its future was further ensured in 1927 with the formation of the Akita Inu Hozankai Society of Japan.

Highly revered by Japanese society it is not uncommon for the family of a newly born baby to be given a small statue of an Akita to signify health, happiness and longevity.

Powerful, athletic and courageous, the Akita is easy to train but can be dominant, bossy and show a stubborn streak making it highly unsuitable for novice owners. Care should be taken when introducing children and other pets although it is possible for the breed to live happily with either.

Dalmatian

Dalmatian		
Breed Group	Utility	
Height	Bitch	56 – 58cm
	Male	58 – 61cm
Weight	Bitch	23 – 25kg
	Male	23 – 25kg
Lifespan	10 –12 years	

ONE OF THE MOST DISTINCTIVE and well known of all breeds, the Dalmatian is a lively and extrovert dog. Spotted dogs like these appeared on many Ancient Greek friezes showing them working with charioteers but it is generally thought that the breed itself originated in northern India before reaching the state of Dalmatia, in what is now southern Croatia, by travelling in

Fun Facts

In the United States, Dalmatians are often known as Firehouse Dogs. In the late 1800s they were used by fire departments to clear a path through the streets for their horse–drawn water wagons.

gypsy caravans in the Middle Ages.

Over the centuries, the Dalmatian has been used in many other roles. It has been a border guard and a hunter, a cart puller and a sheep herder. It has even graced the circus ring. When the breed was introduced into Britain in the eighteenth century, its elegant form, considerable stamina and impressive paces led to it becoming extremely popular with the aristocracy as a coaching dog. Looking highly ornate, the animals would run alongside their master's horse–drawn carriage providing both flamboyant decoration and sharp–toothed protection from highwaymen and robbers.

To own, the Dalmatian is a friendly, confident and outgoing breed of dog. They are dedicated and loyal to their owners but can easily develop mischievous habits if under–exercised or not entertained. Remember, this is a breed of incredible stamina capable of travelling almost indefinitely at a steady pace and, as such needs regular, lengthy walks and opportunities off of the lead.

Shar Pei

Shar Pei		
Breed Group	Utility	
Height	Bitch	46 – 51cm
	Male	46 – 51cm
Weight	Bitch	18kg
	Male	18kg
Lifespan	8 – 10 years	

THE CENTURIES OLD SHAR PEI IS one of the world's most unusual dogs and also one of the rarest. Clay–fired statuettes of a dog very similar in appearance to the Shar Pei have been found that date back to the Han Dynasty (202BC – 206AD). They are believed to have originated from the village of Dah Let in Southern China's Kwangtung Province near Canton – a veritable Las Vegas for gamblers of the

time – where they were a favourite contestant in dog fights.

Breeders, keen to improve the dog's chances, developed some of the characteristics we see in the Shar Pei today – notably its loose, wrinkly skin that made it difficult to grip hold of and allowed the dog to twist and turn without injury. The Shar Pei's popularity, however, started to wane with the introduction of larger and more ferocious dogs from Europe. No longer in demand, breeding was neglected and numbers dwindled.

A further blow to the Shar Pei's survival came in 1947 when the communist government of Chairman Mao, considering the ownership of dogs to be a "decadent bourgeois luxury", increased the tax on ownership and banned all breeding. By the 1950s, the only remaining examples existed on the islands of Macau and Hong Kong.

Fortunately, with the help of Western breeders, the Shar Pei's numbers made a slow but gradual recovery. The first dog arrived in the United Kingdom in 1981 and, since that time, it has flourished. Within four years 350 of the animals were registered with the Kennel Club and now this number exceeds 2,000.

The loving and friendly Shar Pei is a pleasure to own and makes a superb addition to any family. They are exceptionally loyal and devoted and love playing games, especially with children. They can, however, prove a bit of a handful in the presence of other dogs so extra care must be taken on walks and an escape proof garden is a must.

Fun Facts

Like its distant relation the Chow Chowm the Shar Pei's tongue is blue–black in colour.

Poodle

Poodle		
Breed Group	Utility	
Height	Bitch	38cm
	Male	38cm
Weight	Bitch	21 – 32kg
	Male	30 – 35kg
Lifespan	10 – 14 years	

THERE ARE THREE SIZES OF POODLE of which the Standard breed is the largest and oldest. As with so many breeds, its precise origins are unclear but it is most commonly thought that the Poodle heralded first from Germany before being taken to France and other countries by the Landsknechte – mercenary soldiers in the pay of Maximilian I.

The Poodle gradually evolved into its present form in France. They were primarily bred as versatile hunting dogs being nimble, fast of foot and thoroughly adept swimmers – ideal for retrieving game birds from water and marshland. For many breeds this would be activity enough however, the Poodle also found fame in a rather different mode of employment – as a performer! Extremely intelligent, fast to

Fun Facts

There's a new pup in town! Gaining popularity is the Labradoodle – a Labrador/Poodle cross hybrid – the most famous of which is probably TG, the occasional star of BBC television show Top Gear owned by presenter Richard Hammond.

learn and always eager to please it graced the stages, circus rings and pavements of Europe as an accomplished trick artist.

Poodles tend to like everyone and everything. People, pets small and large, children – all are friends to this big hearted dog. Alert and vocal, they can make superb guard dogs but are never aggressive in any way. They are, of course, a fairly large dog used to being out and about so a considerable level of exercise is essential to keep it in good health.

Working Dogs

THE WORKING DOGS GROUP fetures many of the strongest, staminal and skilful of all the canine breeds. As with numerous other dogs, many of them started out as hunting companions but their versatility and endurance led to them being utilised for ever more diverse and varying tasks.

They have become guard dogs, patrol dogs and sentinels – many have served with armed forces and police departments across the world. They have herded cattle, sheep, poultry and even reindeer. They have pulled mail carts and fish wagons in Britain and fur pelts and medical supplies within the Arctic Circle. They have assisted man across deserts and to the North and South Poles. Felons have been tracked, climbers have been rescued and everything has been sniffed out from explosives to contraband to truffles! There can be no doubt that the working dogs know how to work hard.

Rottweiler

THE SUPER–POWERFUL ROTTWEILER'S origins are not totally clear but it is thought that they are descended from a large Mastiff type breed that was used by the Roman legions to safeguard and drove their livestock as they crossed the Alps. By the Middle Ages in the south-west German town of Rottweil, the breed had been crossed with local sheepdogs to produce the Rottweiler Metzgerhund or Rottweil butchers' dog. As with its Roman ancestor, it was first used to drive cattle from town to town until, with the advent of the railways, this practice became illegal in the nine-teenth century.

As a result the Rottweiler suffered an unfortunate decline in popularity and in numbers. This was until 1914 and the start of the First World War when its outstanding strength, stamina and mental capability saw it pressed into service with the German military as a messenger and guard dog. The breed gained prominence in the United Kingdom during the 1930s, finally being accepted by the Kennel Club in 1936.

A Rottweiler can make a superb pet and household guardian in the correct hands and will offer unconditional loyalty and protection to its owner. However, it must always be remembered that this is a temperamental breed – some animals will be friendly, gregarious and outgoing to the last whilst others will show independence and feign disinterest. Above all they can display aggressive tendencies and are, therefore, not suitable for novice or nervous handlers under any circumstances.

Fun Facts

The Rottweiler's special talents as a guard dog have long been recognised. In Medieval times, travelling, wealthy traders would sometimes tie their money–pouches around the neck of their trusty Rottweiler!

Rottweiler		
Breed Group	Working	
Height	Bitch	58 – 64cm
	Male	63 – 69cm
Weight	Bitch	38kg
	Male	50kg
Lifespan	10 – 12 years	

Dobermann

Dobermann		
Breed Group	Working	
Height	Bitch	63 – 68cm
	Male	68 – 72cm
Weight	Bitch	32 – 45kg
	Male	32 – 45kg
Lifespan	12 years	

THE DOBERMANN WAS A RESULT of the life work of Louis Dobermann, a tax collector and night watchman in Apolda in the south–central German state of Thueringen. It is said that he wanted to produce the ultimate guard and protection dog to accompany him on his rounds. Although the exact genetic make–up of the breed remains unknown to this day, it is thought that he used Great Danes and Rottweilers for their inherent size and strength, Greyhounds for their speed and agility and the Manchester Terrier for its tenacity, sleek coat and athletic profile. Other breeds are also said to have contributed including the Weimaraner, German Shorthaired Pointer and the German Shepherd.

The first Dobermann was registered in the German Studbook in 1893 before gaining full German Kennel Club recognition in 1900. Unsurprisingly, the breed was called into service during the First World War for guard and patrol work and has since been utilised by police forces and the military the world over.

Supremely intelligent, loyal and affectionate a Dobermann can become an outstanding household pet although it must always be remembered that they

were originally bred to be a strong and aggressive guardian of person and property. Firm handling is a must from the outset with the breed responding better to a strong voice and firm will. They are highly energetic dogs that require time, devotion and, above all, confidence. If you are not able to provide all three then the Dobermann is not the dog for you.

Boxer

Boxer		
Breed Group	Working	
Height	Bitch	53 – 59cm
	Male	57 – 63cm
Weight	Bitch	25 – 27kg
	Male	30 – 32kg
Lifespan	7 – 10 years	

THE PETER PAN OF THE CANINE world, the Boxer is a breed that just refuses to grow up – young or old it is always ready to play a game. Created in Germany in the latter half of the nineteenth century it is descended from the now extinct Bullenbeisser and Bärenbeisse – two stocky Mastiff types that were bred extensively in Germany during the Middle Ages and used for the hunting of boar, bear and deer and for bull baiting – which were interbred with Bulldogs that were imported from England to create the happy–go–lucky breed we know and love today.

Seen in all shades from red to fawn, brindle or even white the Boxer makes a great, fun–filled family pet. They are very quick to learn, eager to please and

extremely courageous and loyal. It should, however always be remembered that whilst they preserve their puppyish charm throughout their years they also retain their juvenile mentality and, as such, can be chaotic and a bit of a handful. They love to be kept busy and do not respond to being left alone at home for extended periods of time – if nothing else this is guaranteed to bring out a Boxer's destructive tendencies.

Great Dane

Great Dane		
Breed Group	Working	
Height	Bitch	71 – 76cm
	Male	76 – 81cm
Weight	Bitch	26 – 54kg
	Male	54 – 62kg
Lifespan	5 – 10 years	

DESPITE ITS IMMENSE SIZE THE Great Dane is truly a gentle giant of the canine world.

Similar large Mastiff type dogs have existed for several millennia and can be seen in ancient Egyptian drawings dating back to 2200BC. These large dogs are believed to have travelled across Europe and Asia with merchants, traders and soldiers from where they formed the basis of many of the common breeds of dog we know today. It was, however, in Germany during the Middle Ages that the Great Dane itself was finally developed following a period of cross breeding with Greyhounds – this breed is thought to have given the Dane its characteristic deep chest, slender body and surprising agility.

They were first used as bull–baiters but, with their immense size, soon became seen as a status symbol amongst the nobility who would use them in the field for the hunting of wild boar. It is variously known as the Deutsche Dogge (German Mastiff), Grand Danois or the Dänisches Hund (Danish Dog).

Perhaps the most important thing to bear in mind when considering a Great

Dane as a pet is whether you have the space! Only by meeting one face to face can you truly appreciate the size of this magnificent creature – on their back legs they tower over almost any human. Despite its enormity, the Great Dane is a quiet, affectionate and intelligent dog that can become very loyal to its owner and their family and seeks little more than a warm and snug place to lay its head at night.

Fun Facts

Disney might have us believe that the largest dog in the world was called Digby but the real holder of that impressive accolade is Gibson the Harlequin Great Dane. Bred in the United States he stands 107cm to the shoulder and almost 220cm when standing on his hind legs.

Siberian Husky

THERE CAN BE FEW PEOPLE UN-aware of the impressive feats of endurance performed by the Siberian Husky. Perfectly tuned for the harsh Arctic conditions, the breed originated near the Kolyma River in the east of Siberia during the nineteenth century where it was employed by the nomadic Chukchi people not only as a sled dog but also for reindeer herding and as a watchdog.

Still known as the Chukchi dog, the first huskies arrived in Alaska and Canada with fur traders as recently as the early part of the twentieth century where their speed and stamina quickly gained them universal favour and they were renamed the Siberian Husky.

The Siberian Husky came to national fame in 1925 when it was realised that a Diphtheria epidemic was about to take hold in Nome, Alaska with the only supplies of anti–toxin held in Anchorage some 1,085 km away. Harsh conditions prevented the use of aircraft so a dog–sled relay was instigated. Several teams were used, the most famous being those of Gunnar Kaasan and Leonhard Seppala. A statue of Balto, the lead dog of the final relay, commemorates the achievement of all the dogs and mush-

Siberian Husky		
Breed Group	Working	
Height	Bitch	51 – 56cm
	Male	53 – 60cm
Weight	Bitch	16 – 23kg
	Male	20 – 27kg
Lifespan	16 years +	

ers in the 1925 Serum Run and is displayed in New York's Central Park.

With a calm temperament and naturally calm nature the Siberian Husky can make an excellent family pet. They adore people and thrive on company but often display a mind of their own – a well–fenced garden is essential to prevent them going off on any unplanned adventures. Whilst they are not inclined to bark they do like to howl – often just for the sheer pleasure of it!

Fun Facts

The strongest Husky and, in fact, the strongest dog of all time was Charlie who, in 1963, pulled a 1425kg sled without any other assistance.

Other books also available:

Greatest
MOMENTS OF
GRAND PRIX
by JON SPROON

Featuring 22 of the Classic Moments of GRAND PRIX

Greatest
MOMENTS OF
BOXING
by IAN WELCH

Featuring 22 of the Classic Moments of BOXING

Greatest
MOMENTS OF
CRICKET
by RALPH DELLOR and STEPHEN LAMB

Featuring 30 of the Classic Moments of CRICKET

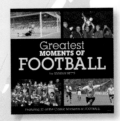
Greatest
MOMENTS OF
FOOTBALL
by GRAHAM BETTS

Featuring 22 of the Classic Moments of FOOTBALL

Greatest
MOMENTS OF
RUGBY
by IAN WELCH

Featuring 22 of the Classic Moments of RUGBY

Greatest
MOMENTS OF
SNOOKER
by IAN WELCH

Featuring 22 of the Classic Moments of SNOOKER

Greatest
MOMENTS OF
GOLF
by BILL CARTER

Featuring 30 of the Classic Moments of GOLF

THE LITTLE BOOK OF
FOOTBALL

LITTLE BOOK OF THE
SIX NATIONS
By Graeme Kent

THE LITTLE BOOK OF
WELSH RUGBY
Written by
Andy Howell
2nd

THE LITTLE BOOK OF
CRICKET
WORLD CUP SPECIAL EDITION
Written by Ralph Dellor and Stephen Lamb

THE LITTLE BOOK OF
GOLF

Available from all major stockists

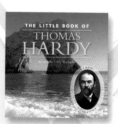

Available from all major stockists

The pictures in this book were provided courtesy of the following:

GETTY IMAGES
101 Bayham Street, London NW1 0AG

SHUTTERSTOCK
www.stutterstock.com

JON STROUD

Design and artwork by David Wildish

Creative Director Kevin Gardner

Published by Green Umbrella Publishing

Publishers Jules Gammond and Vanessa Gardner

Written by Jon Stroud